A Day in the Life: Polar Animals

Narwhal

Katie Marsico

Heinemann Library
Chicago, Illinois

www.capstonepub.com
Visit our website to find out more information about Heinemann-Raintree books

To order:
☎ Phone 800-747-4992
💻 Visit www.capstonepub.com to browse our catalog and order online.

Edited by Rebecca Rissman, Daniel Nunn, and Sian Smith
Designed by Joanna Hinton-Malivoire
Picture research by Hannah Taylor
Originated by Capstone Global Library Ltd
Printed and bound in the United States of America in North Mankato, Minnesota.
042017   010434RP

19 18 17
10 9 8 7

Library of Congress Cataloging-in-Publication Data
Marsico, Katie, 1980-
  Narwhal / Katie Marsico.
    p. cm.—(A day in the life : polar animals)
  Includes bibliographical references and index.
ISBN 978-1-4329-5332-4 (hc)
ISBN 978-1-4329-5339-3 (pb)
1. Narwhal—Juvenile literature. I. Title.
  QL737.C433K38 2012
  599.5'43—dc22   2010050019

Acknowledgments
We would like to thank the following for permission to reproduce photographs: Corbis p. 6 (Paul Nicklen); FLPA pp. 4 (Minden Pictures/ Flip Nicklin), 7, 23c (Minden Pictures/ Flip Nicklin), 11 (Minden Pictures/ Flip Nicklin), 12 (Minden Pictures/ Flip Nicklin), 17 (Sunset), 19 (Minden Pictures/ Flip Nicklin), 22 (Minden Pictures/ Flip Nicklin); Getty Images pp. 5, 23g (Paul Nicklen), 8, 23b (Paul Nicklen), 9 (Rudi Sebastian), 16 (Minden Pictures/ Flip Nicklin), 18 (Minden Pictures/Flip Nicklin), 20, 23d (Minden Pictures/Flip Nicklin), 21 (Minden Pictures/Flip Nicklin); Photolibrary pp. 13, 23f (Waterframe Images), 14 (Robert Harding), 15 (Oxford Scientific/Doug Allan); SeaPics.com pp. 10, 23a (© John K.B. Ford/Ursus).

Front cover photograph of a narwhal and back cover photograph of a narwhal's tusk reproduced with permission of Getty Images (Paul Nicklen). Back cover photograph of a tail reproduced with permission of Corbis (Paul Nicklen).

The publisher would like to thank Michael Bright for his assistance in the preparation of this book.

Every effort has been made to contact copyright holders of material reproduced in this book. Any omissions will be rectified in subsequent printings if notice is given to the publisher.

Contents

Some words are shown in bold, **like this**.
You can find them in the glossary on page 23.

A narwhal is a **mammal** that lives in icy **polar** waters.

All mammals have some hair on their bodies and feed their babies milk.

tusk

Narwhals are whales.

Males have a long tooth called a **tusk** on their upper jaw.

What Does a Narwhal Look Like?

tail

Narwhals have flippers and a tail.

Most have spotted skin.

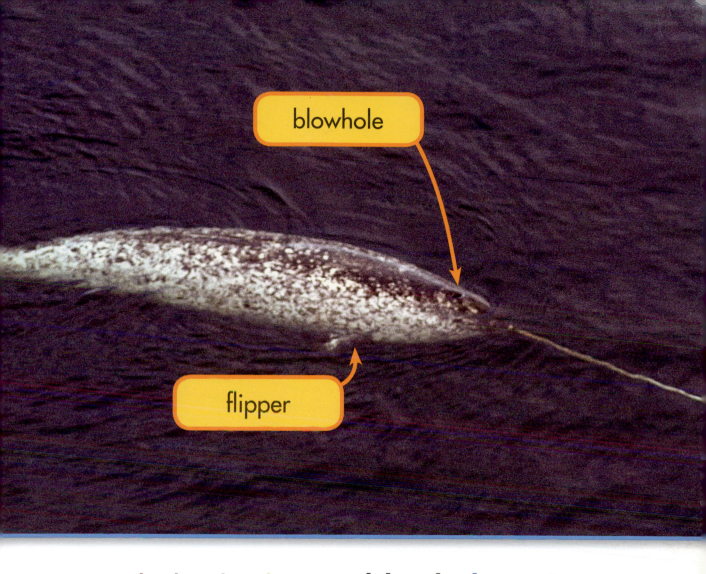

blowhole

flipper

Narwhals also have a **blowhole** at the top of their head.

They use the blowhole to breathe in air at the surface of the water.

Arctic

Narwhals live in the **Arctic**.

In the Arctic it is light all day and all night for part of the summer.

In the Arctic it is dark all day and all night for part of the winter.

The Arctic is one of the coldest places in the world!

What Does a Narwhal Do in the Day?

Narwhals are **active** during the day and at night.

They spend part of the day searching for food deep in the ocean.

Narwhals spend some time resting near the surface of the water.

They need to breathe in air before they dive down to search for food.

fish

Narwhals eat fish, shrimp, and squid.

They often catch their food deep in the ocean, where it is very dark.

12

Narwhals make sounds that bounce back and tell them where things are.

This is called **sonar**.

killer whale

Killer whales hunt and eat narwhals.

Polar bears and walruses also
attack them.

People hunt narwhals, too.

They kill the whales for their **tusks** and skin.

Narwhals live in groups called pods.

This helps them to keep safe from
their enemies.

There are usually about 15 to 20 narwhals in a pod.

Narwhals travel together and communicate by using sounds such as clicks and whistles.

What Do Narwhals Do at Night?

Narwhals spend a lot of the night diving for food.

They can dive down into very deep parts of the ocean.

Narwhals sometimes rest in between dives at night, just as they do in the day.

People are still trying to find out more about how narwhals sleep.

What Are Baby Narwhals Like?

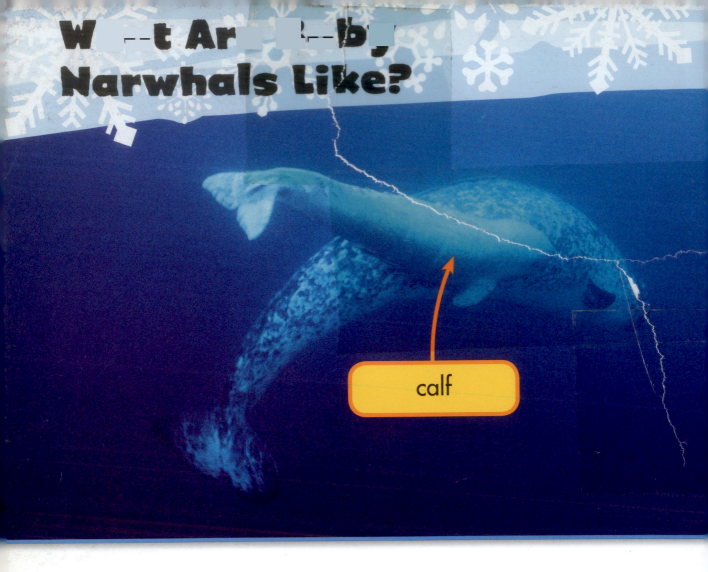

calf

A mother narwhal gives birth to a baby about once every three years.

Baby narwhals are called calves. They are a blue-gray color.

A calf lives with its mother for one or two years while it drinks her milk.

Then young narwhals are ready to join a pod and go hunting in icy waters!

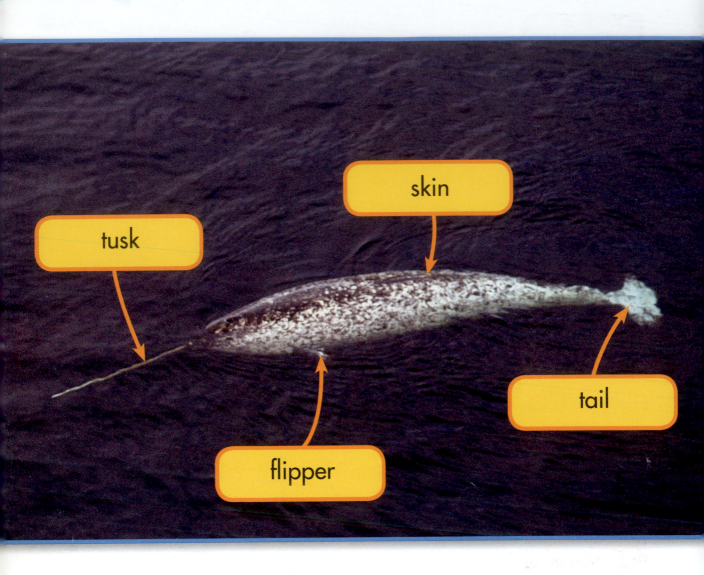

tusk

skin

flipper

tail

Glossary

 **active** busy doing lots of things

 **Arctic** area surrounding the North Pole. It is very cold in the Arctic.

 **blowhole** hole at the top of a narwhal's head used for breathing air

 **mammal** animal that feeds its babies milk. All mammals have some hair or fur on their bodies.

 **polar** extremely cold areas at the top and bottom of the world

 **sonar** a system that uses sound to find objects

 **tusk** long, pointed tooth

Books

Halfmann, Janet. *Narwhal: Unicorn of the Sea*. Norwalk, CT: Soundprints Division of Trudy Corporation, 2009.

Swan Miller, Sara. *Whales of the Arctic*. New York City: PowerKids Press, 2009.

Websites

video.kids.nationalgeographic.com/video/player/kids/animals-pets-kids/wild-detectives-kids/wd-ep4-narwhaltooth.html

Watch a video of narwhals on the National Geographic Website.

www.sciencenewsforkids.org/articles/20060125/Feature1.asp

Find out about a narwhal's tooth at Science News for Kids.

Index